A Foster Child Comes to Stay with Josie and Brooke

By Cheryl Petersen

Illustrated by Tanya Stewart

Copyright © 2002 by Cheryl
Petersen
ISBN: 978-0-9795454-2-9
0-9795454-2-0

Published by Neutrino
Publishing

Library of Congress Catalog
Card No.: 01-126864

Quotes from: New American Standard Bible NASB
Copyright © 1960 - 1995 by The Lockman Foundation.

For permissions:
www.HealingScienceToday.com

__Introduction__

Hi,
In this true story, Josie and Brooke learn about fostering.

Two-year old Junior came to live at their home. Junior became a good friend and like a brother.

Foster children are the same as other children.

After Junior returned to live with his mom, Josie and Brooke lived with foster girls who became good friends and like sisters.

Fostering showed that we can be one big family.

Josie and Brooke are sisters.
They live on a farm with their
mom and dad. Josie is tall and
strong, always trying to do
things on her own. Brooke,
who is three years younger, is
petite and thoughtful, but
full of spunk. She easily
keeps up with Josie.

Like most sisters, they occasionally have disagreements. But, they try to solve problems with Love. It helps them get along better. And when things change, Love is there to help them do their best.

One day, Mom and Dad told the sisters that a little boy was going to come live with them. He was going to share their bedroom. His name was Junior.

Junior needed a foster home. His mom was not able to take care of him for a while. And Junior didn't know his dad.

That night, the girls were in their bedroom. Josie was wondering why Junior had to stay with them in their little house. Where would his crib fit? But, looking around the room, Josie realized that a crib would fit in the corner if they moved her dresser into the closet.

Brooke however, was thinking about something else. What would it feel like not to have a mom and dad around all the time? She didn't want to know.

When Junior came, he wouldn't talk. Josie and Brooke tried to make him feel at home. They tried to share stuffed animals with Junior. They asked Junior many questions, but still he would not talk. They took him outside and showed him the swing set. From the smile on his face, they could tell he liked being there. So they stayed with him.

Junior and the sisters were happily playing outside. Then, Dad drove up to the house on his four-wheeler motorcycle. Junior got very scared. Not only did the noise bother him, but Dad did too. For some reason, Junior was not comfortable around Dad. Junior ran to Mom in the house. Mom calmed Junior down and let him help her prepare dinner.

Bedtime was prayer time for Josie and Brooke. Mom came into the bedroom to say prayers, too. Junior listened quietly and smiled as they began repeating a prayer given by Christ Jesus. "Our Father who is in heaven." The sisters looked at Junior and knew God was his Parent. They finished the prayer. "Hallowed be Your name. Your Kingdom come. Your will be done, on earth as it is in heaven. Give us this day our daily bread. And forgive us our debts, as we also have forgiven our debtors. And do not lead us into temptation, but deliver us from evil. [For Yours is the kingdom and the power and the glory forever]." (Matt. 6:9, NASB)

Over the next few days, the family discovered that many other noises and things scared Junior.

The family learned from the Bible that God's love gets rid of fear (I John 4:18). They wanted to be more thoughtful, like God. They had to do things differently. Do things according to Love and not habit. For example, Josie and Brooke would take Junior outside to play when Mom used the noisy vacuum. And, when Junior would easily get afraid, they stopped what they were doing and took the time to calm him patiently.

Within a few weeks, Junior's fears were going away. Even Dad did not frighten him anymore. Everyone felt happier.

Late one night, Junior woke up crying. Mom came into the room and picked him up. She could tell his ear was hurting. Mom sat down on the floor and hugged Junior.

By now the sisters started to wake. They could hear Mom whisper the words to another one of their favorite prayers, written by Mary Baker Eddy:

Father-Mother God.
Loving me.
Guard me when I sleep;
Guide my little feet
Up to Thee.

Junior quickly quieted down and fell asleep. Mom continued to pray.

Josie and Brooke did not know
how long Mom stayed in the
room because they fell back to
sleep.

Junior slept through the night.
The next morning, Junior woke
up very happy. His ear had
drained. God is not just a
Father, but also a Mother,
protecting, guiding and
comforting everyone.

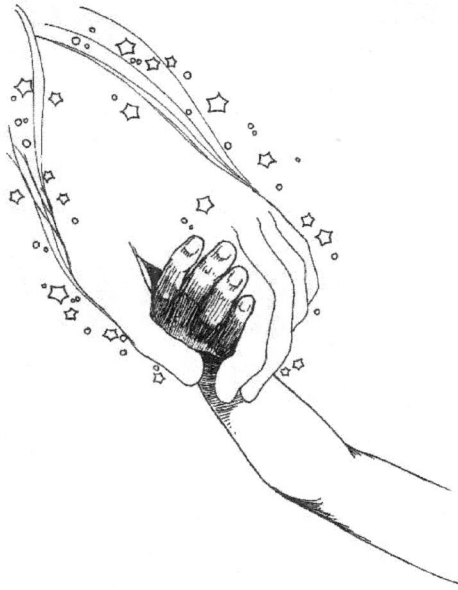

It wasn't long before Junior began talking. "Motorcycle" was his first word. He even let Dad take him for a ride on the four-wheeler!

A year later, Junior's mom was able to take him back to their house. Josie and Brooke were glad to know we can change for the better and feel the love of one big family.

www.ingramcontent.com/pod-product-compliance
Lightning Source LLC
Chambersburg PA
CBHW060606030426
42337CB00019B/3636